MONTHLY BULLETIN

OF

The Fidelity and Casualty Company

OF NEW YORK

FOR THE INFORMATION OF ITS AGENTS

| VOLUME XVI | JANUARY, 1911 | NUMBER 1 |

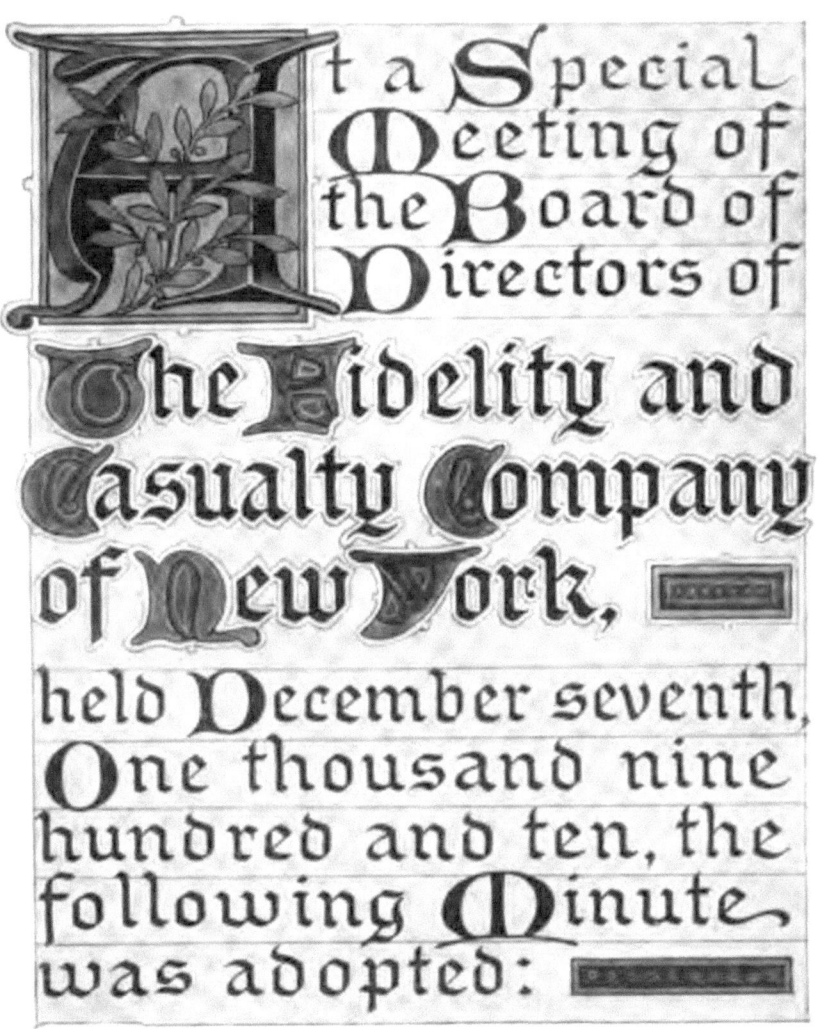

At a Special Meeting of the Board of Directors of The Fidelity and Casualty Company of New York, held December seventh, One thousand nine hundred and ten, the following Minute was adopted:

In the interest of creating a more extensive selection of rare historical book reprints, we have chosen to reproduce this title even though it may possibly have occasional imperfections such as missing and blurred pages, missing text, poor pictures, markings, dark backgrounds and other reproduction issues beyond our control. Because this work is culturally important, we have made it available as a part of our commitment to protecting, preserving and promoting the world's literature. Thank you for your understanding.

MONTHLY BULLETIN

OF

The Fidelity and Casualty Company

OF NEW YORK

NEW YORK, JANUARY, 1911

IN MEMORIAM

We offer this number of the MONTHLY BULLETIN as a memorial to the life and work of our late president, Hon. George F. Seward, who departed this life on the 28th of November, 1910, a little before nine o'clock in the morning.

However warm our hearts, however earnest our intentions, and however diligent our endeavors, we recognize the absolute futility of attempting to present to our representatives in the field a memorial adequate to the merits of so great a man. We, probably to a greater extent than those who may be our critics, recognize the inadequacy and shortcomings of this slight token of our regard that we would offer in memory of our departed chief.

In the words of Robert Browning, he was

"One who never turned his back, but march'd breast forward,
Never doubted clouds would break,
Never dream'd though right were worsted, wrong would triumph,
Held we fall to rise, are baffled to fight better, sleep to wake."

Nowhere, we believe, can there be found words as succinct and adequate as these in their direct application to the character of Mr. Seward. It is as though Browning had known him intimately for years and had written these lines as an epitaph.

The subject of our memorial was endowed with heroic courage—a courage that might seem to be native only to the heroic times of mythology rather than to the matter-of-fact, give and take, commercial life of the present day.

His was a courage of his convictions, and, we believe, those convictions were nearly always right; for he never arrived at them until after hearing patiently all the arguments from those best qualified to present their opposing cases, and until after he had focused the rays of his own incisive and synthetic mind upon the proposition like the burning rays of the sun through a monumental sun-glass. And, thus focused, like the rays of the sun, his intellect burned its way through the jumbled tissues of the fabric of fallacy and inaccuracy. Furthermore, on behalf of the purity of his convictions, not only would he not brook inaccurate statements and fallacious arguments, but he guarded assiduously the fountain springs of information and the channels through which such information flowed to him. He thus fortified his convictions—to change the figure of speech—with a rampart of rules of evidence that almost completely shut out false premises which would make possible erroneous judgment.

It may be said, consequently, that his courage and convictions were closely co-related and interdependent. He was courageous because he was sure of his convictions; he had convictions because he had indomitable courage. Once his mind was made up as to what was right or what was wrong he "never turned his back, but march'd breast forward."

Once his ideas crystallized themselves into convictions, he was ready to meet in single combat, if necessary, whatever opponents might spring up across his path. Nor did he look for a well-trodden path to the goal of his ambitions, but like an explorer through the dense, miasmic underbrush of the tropics, he expected to hew his way. At these times, although essentially aggressive, he was nevertheless a fair fighter, conducting his campaign at all times and under all circumstances according to the most exacting demands of the ethics of fair play. And after the conflict was at an end and the victory was his, vanquished opponents found him the fairest man with whom to arrange terms of capitulation.

Even though for the time being he might suffer apparent defeat, yet his courage was so great that he fought on, believing never that "though right were worsted, wrong would triumph"; holding that "we fall to rise, are baffled to fight better, sleep to wake."

We have laid stress upon Mr. Seward's indomitable courage, stalwart convictions, and aggressive militancy. They were certainly the characteristics most prominently minted upon the gold coin of his character. They stood out upon the metal sharply outlined in every detail, assuring the genuineness of the coin and giving it currency wherever men place a value upon character.

Other characteristics of hardly secondary importance were mental alertness, keen analytic powers, concentration of mental faculties, and business acumen.

Even to those who knew him best and longest Mr. Seward's alertness of mind was a continual marvel. His ability to take in immediately the essentials of an abstruse proposition inspired in the observer only less admiration than his ability to pass from that proposition to an entirely different and equally difficult one without a moment's notice. To the solution of every proposition, however diverse of character, he seemed to marshal his mental faculties unblinded with the dust stirred up by the previous heated arguments. He entered upon the consideration of a new proposition with a free and untrammelled mind.

We have already claimed for Mr. Seward that he had a synthetic mind—a mind peculiarly adapted to construct a principle out of a mass of none too closely related details. He could go over a mass of details, or listen to a statement involving numerous facts, pick the essentials, and lay out unerringly the right line of action or construct a general governing principle. But his mind was more than synthetic—it was analytic as well. He could take a proposition brought to him for his acceptance, and in a marvelously short time separate it into its original elements, and by so doing satisfy not only himself as to its soundness or fallacy, but likewise him who stood sponsor for it.

Inferior to none of these qualities, we believe, was that of concentration of mind upon the matter in hand. Even the most casual observer, has had this faculty of Mr. Seward's indelibly impressed upon his memory. When writing an article or examining a written proposition, Mr. Seward seemed to be oblivious to all external things. His mind seemed, at such times, encased in an absolutely sound- and vision-proof compartment. Conversation could go on around him, typewriters might click, elevated trains might pass the open windows, or the office-boy might inject his ubiquitous personality right under his eyes—but all these things seemed at such times never to reach Mr. Seward's consciousness. He never showed any irritation under such circumstances; it was only when illogical or incorrect statements, surplusage of words, or rambling expositions, interfered with the logical development of the argument at hand that he was likely to show a degree of impatience. He could stand confusion as long as it did not concern the matter that he had under consideration; but confusion of whatever kind when injected into the subject at hand, he could not tolerate.

To say that Mr. Seward had business acumen is to state a truism. The prominent position held by this corporation in the casualty insurance world is satisfactory evidence of that fact. The Fidelity and Casualty Company is his masterpiece. When he became vice-president in 1887, the company was rather a small institution struggling valiantly for a place in the casualty insurance world under the banner of the now victorious principle of multiple line business. Two years before, the assets of the company were set down as $575,000, and the volume of business done, about $450,000. On the 31st of December last, the assets were approximately $9,600,000 and the amount of business written $7,915,412.79. These figures speak far more eloquently of the business ability of Mr. Seward than could many words; and we need not develop the point any further than to add that the greatest triumph scored by him during this period of almost unexampled prosperity for the company was the final practically unqualified acceptance by competitors of the soundness of the principle of multiple lines in the casualty insurance business. Strange to say, he had to fight for every inch of ground before this principle was even tacitly recognized. Every avenue leading to its acceptance was disputed by powerful competitors, who more than once were dangerously near the accomplishment of their purpose, namely, the destruction of this company. He had to fight his opponents in the legislature of nearly every state in which the company did business; and the battle was waged at times not merely to gain ground, but literally to prevent annihilation. But Mr. Seward had what must have been the exquisite pleasure of seeing nearly all of his competitors come around to his point of view. Nearly every month now witnesses single line casualty companies taking on additional lines, and, it is reported, that several companies deepest dyed in the single line wool are discussing rather seriously the advisability of enlarging the scope of their activities.

There was another side to Mr. Seward's personality that the casual observer could not have known, and that even those who were better acquainted with him might have thought inconsistent with those qualities to which we have devoted the major part of this sketch. We refer to his warmth of heart, tenderness of feeling, and breadth of sympathy.

There were those who, after a casual acquaintance or a superficial analysis of his character, thought him cold or somewhat unapproachable. This might be a natural mistake on the part of those who did not know him well, by reason of the fact that he subjected every business proposition presented to him to the keenest kind of logical analysis and always maintained his dignity, whatever the occasion, thus commanding that respect due his position. As far as we are aware, no one ever claimed an acquaintance with him bordering upon familiarity. He had great reserve and, during business hours at least, gave himself up almost entirely to the more serious things of life.

But we who knew him best—we who saw him under those trying conditions when depth of feeling, breadth of sympathy, and charitable action were demanded, know what a warm heart beat within a seemingly steel-hard exterior. When sore affliction befell any of us in this office, Mr. Seward was one of the first, figuratively speaking, to extend a hand in sympathy. What he said, or more particularly what he did, smacked nothing of the ostentatious. Probably a word or two, possibly no words at all—merely a look of deep significance; but his actions, when deeds were necessary, spoke more eloquently than could volumes of effusive words. It was then that the wonderful humanness of the man impressed itself upon one.

Of indomitable will; sagacious and incorruptible; high-minded and true-hearted: Mr. Seward was the kind of man the world has need of. Well might he have said, with the Apostle,

"I have fought a good fight, I have finished my course, I have kept the faith."

May he rest in peace.

GEORGE FREDERICK SEWARD

In the May, 1909, issue of *Assurance*, Mr. Edson S. Lott, President of the United States Casualty Company, wrote an "Appreciation" of Mr. Seward under the caption "Builders of the Casualty Business." That part of Mr. Lott's article of the nature of a character sketch, we shall quote in another part of this memorial issue. From that part essentially biographical, however, we take the liberty of quoting a number of paragraphs, inasmuch as it is the most complete sketch, we believe, that has as yet been printed. After these quotations, we then bring the biography down to date.

Ancestry

"George Frederick Seward was born in the village of Florida, Orange County, N. Y., November 8, 1840, in the house renowned as the birthplace of William H. Seward, Lincoln's great Secretary. [A picture of this house is printed on another page of this issue of the BULLETIN.]

The family name of Seward was first borne in this country by a native of England, who came hither in colonial times. It is a name which holds an illustrious place in American history.

Col. John Seward, the great-grandfather of George F. Seward, was a prominent American officer in the struggle for independence. His son, Dr. Samuel S. Seward, of Sussex, Va., settled in Orange County, New York, after the Revolution, and built up an extensive business, while at the same time practising his profession. He was one of the lay judges of the State under the system then in vogue.

Secretary William H. Seward was a son of the doctor, and is survived by two sons, Frederick W. Seward and Gen. William H. Seward. Another son of the doctor was George W. Seward, the father of George F. Seward.

Mr. Seward received his early education at the Seward Institute, which had been founded by his grandfather. When not quite fifteen years of age he entered Union College at Schenectady, N. Y., but was obliged to leave before the end of the term to assume the direction of his family's landed estate. Such capacity and judgment did he show in the management of this difficult work that by the time he came to his majority he was recognized in his neighborhood as a young man of great promise.

Consular Service in China

In 1861 he was appointed United States Consul to Shanghai, China. [We show on another page a picture of the consulate at Shanghai which was built during Mr. Seward's incumbency of the office and under his supervision.]

This must be regarded as a very important position when one considers what heavy responsibilities were at that time incident to consulship in China. The consuls then had, and in considerable measure still have, jurisdiction, broad in scope and generally discretionary as to its exercise, over all Americans coming to China. The consul was frequently 'judge, jury, and executioner,' and the cases that came before him ranged in character from petty breaches of the peace to murder and piracy—in fact, they covered the whole field of practical jurisprudence.

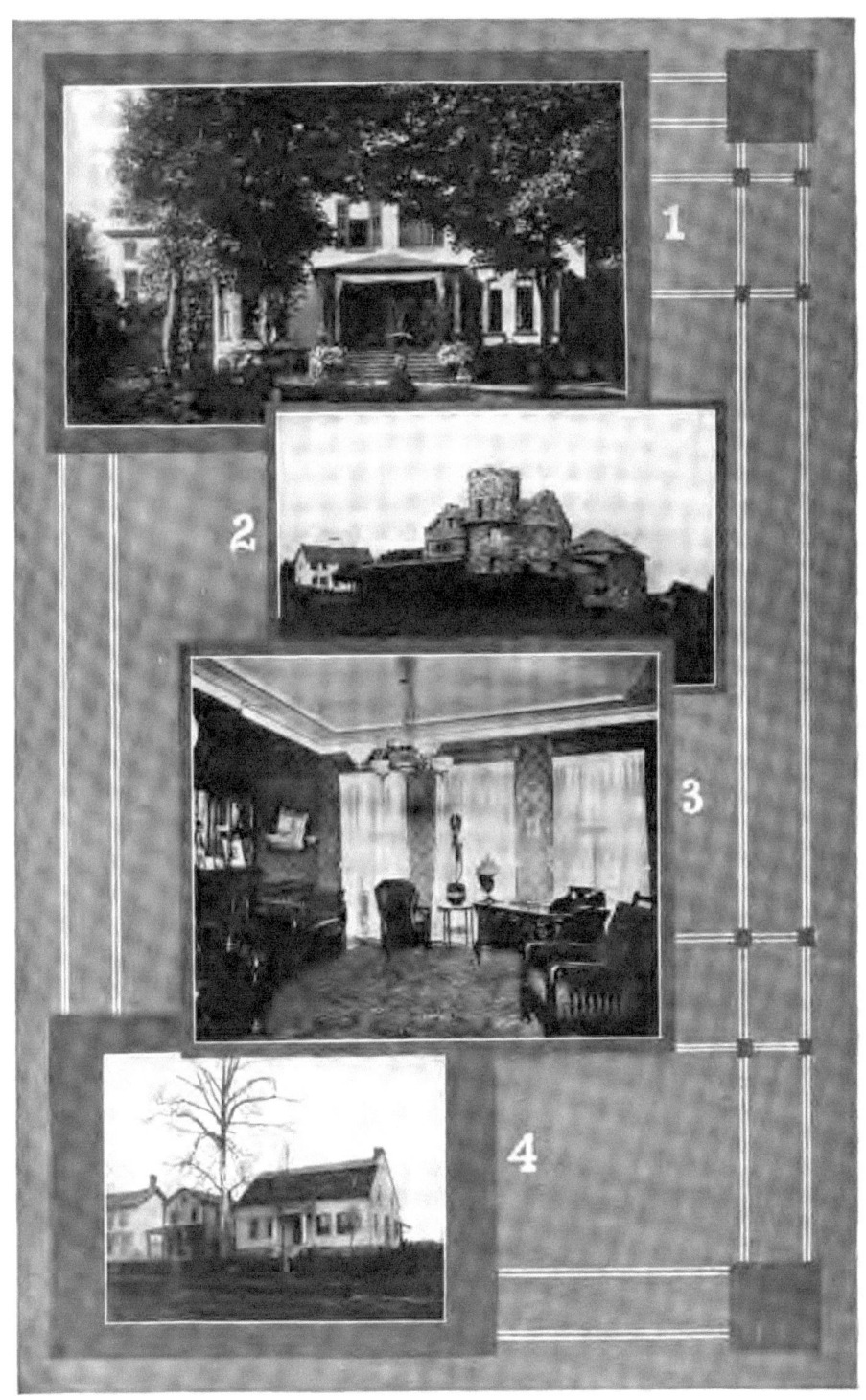

2. Cottage in which Mr. Seward spent a summer at Kennebunkport, Me.
3. Library in Mr. Seward's residence at 136 West 73d Street, New York
4. House in which Mr. Seward was born, Florida, N. Y.
1. Auburn, N. Y., residence of William H. Seward, Secretary of State under Lincoln

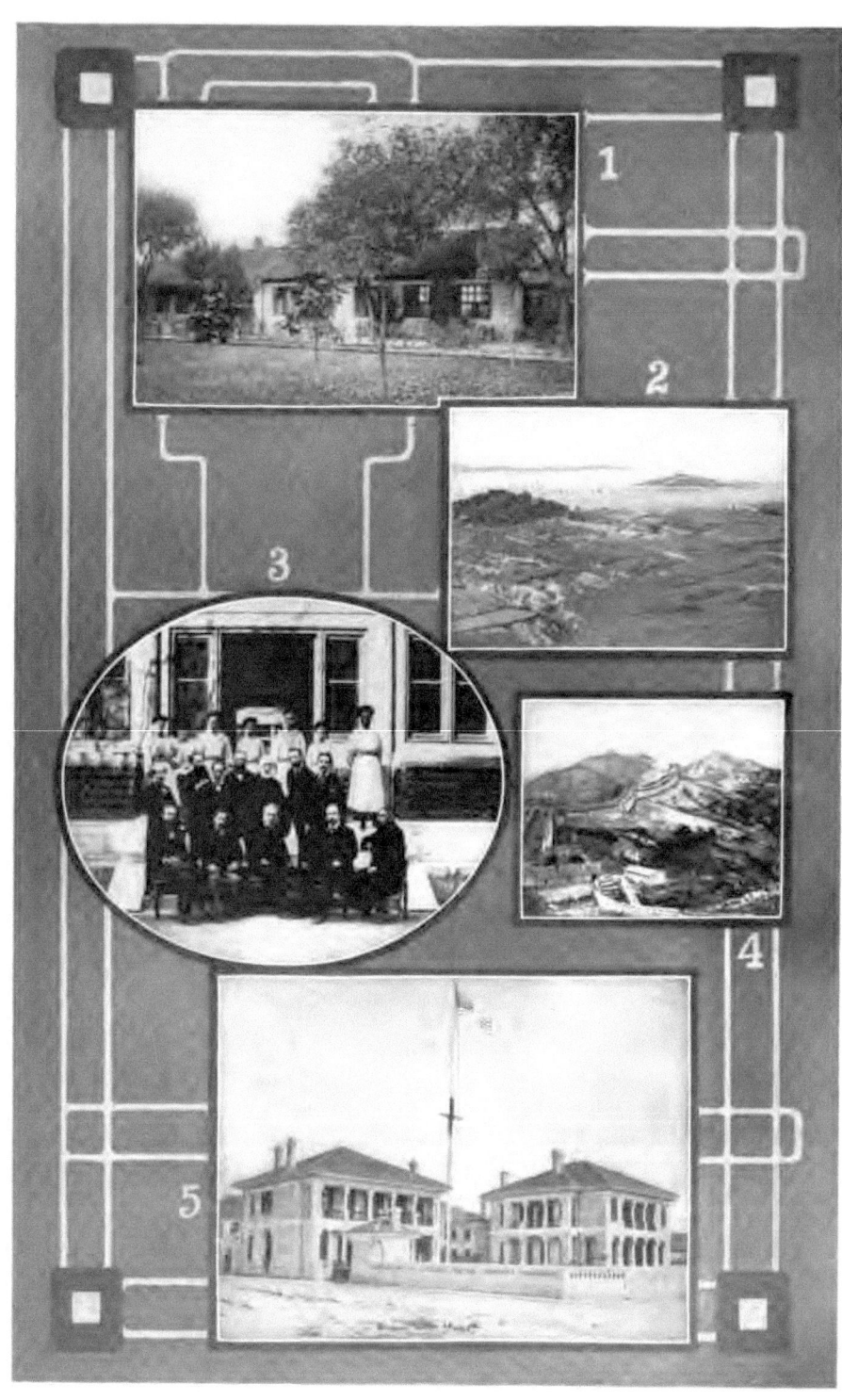

1. Legation at Peking when Mr. Seward was Minister to China
2. Chefoo, treaty port, where Mr. Seward spent his summers while Minister to China
3. Diplomatic Corps at Peking (about 1877) when Mr. Seward was Minister
4. Great Wall of China where Mr. and Mrs. Seward frequently rode horseback
5. U. S. Consulate built by Mr. Seward when Consul-General at Shanghai

Mr. Seward was in China during the most critical and momentous period in that country's modern history. He was there during the careers of Gen. F. T. Ward and 'Chinese' Gordon—the latter of whom was destined to end his life and career in the Soudan. The troops which they commanded operated with the regular soldiers of the empire in putting down the great Taiping Rebellion which had broken out in China; and it was largely through these operations that they afterward gained their wide reputation.

General Gordon (he was at that time Lieutenant-Colonel of Engineers), in a letter addressed on November 7, 1866, to Charles Francis Adams, then United States Minister at the Court of St. James, wrote of Mr. Seward as follows:

'Mr. Seward was placed in extremely difficult circumstances in China in the matter of Burgevine. His liberal and honorable manner of dealing with both of us I felt very much; and it is to his liberal views in this matter that I attribute a great deal of my success; for, had he acted in a narrow-spirited way, the issue of events might have been very different. Of course, these matters are but little known outside of the distant land they take place in, but affecting, as they do, the well-being of many of our fellow-creatures, Your Excellency will excuse my mentioning how much I am indebted to Mr. Seward for the liberal policy he pursued in a very difficult matter.'

The turbulent condition of affairs in China, it will be readily seen, threw a great deal of work upon the young consul, and his duties were more than usually grave and important. Among the criminals brought before Mr. Seward from time to time for trial, were pirates who claimed to be Americans. In his treatment of criminals of this class Mr. Seward showed wisdom and courage. He was obliged to take drastic action in the case of several of these desperadoes, and the energy of his course was commended by United States Minister Burlingame and by Sir Frederick Bruce, British Minister at Peking, in despatches to their respective governments.

In 1864 he was made Consul-General of the United States for all China, and in that capacity showed great creative and executive faculties in his organization of the American consuls in that Empire into an effective and respectable body. About the same time he became Dean of all foreign consuls at Shanghai—a position of honor and responsibility. The following year Mr. Seward was honored by being chosen president of the North China Branch of the Royal Asiatic Society.

Minister to Corea

In 1867 the Administration recognized his work in China by appointing him Minister-Plenipotentiary to Corea, but upon his own representations that the moment for assuming this work was inopportune, the mission was not undertaken. He nevertheless took great interest in Corean affairs; and, in fact, it was he who introduced the movement which ultimately resulted in opening that empire to American commerce.

In 1868 Mr. Seward was sent to Siam to disentangle the knots that had unfortunately been drawn tight in the construction of the treaty between the United States and that country. He was successful in this mission.

Shortly after his return in 1873 from one of his visits to the United States, Mr. Seward was instrumental in quelling with a strong hand a dangerous riot at Shanghai. For a full story of this riot, and Mr. Seward's efforts in putting it down, the reader is referred to the despatch to the State Department in Washington, written by S. Wells Williams, author of 'Middle Kingdom,' then in charge of the United States legation. For this service Mr. Seward received the decoration of the Order of Annam from the French Republic.

In 1874 he was able to carry to a successful conclusion negotiations with the Chinese authorities, giving admission and security to a system of telegraphs and cables established by a Danish company along the coast of China. For this service the King of Denmark created him a Knight Commander of Danebrog—the Grand Cross of the Order being awarded.

Minister to China

At the end of 1875 he was appointed United States Minister at Peking, and held the post until the close of 1880. [A photograph of the embassy at Peking, where Mr. Seward lived, will be seen on another page.]

In the latter year he resigned his place to make way for agents selected by the Administration to undertake the negotiation of a treaty restricting Chinese emigration. This duty he had advised the government he was unwilling to undertake.

While in the diplomatic service in China, Mr. Seward made a number of trips to the United States in the interests of a better consular service. One of these trips was made in 1866; but inasmuch as he arrived in the midst of the troublous events that characterized the close of President Johnson's administration, he found it inexpedient to press his recommendations. He returned in 1869, when he succeeded in having his recommendations accepted by the Administration and enacted into law by Congress.

Contributions to the Literature upon China

Upon his return to America, Mr. Seward placed the rich resources of his experiences in the Orient at the command of those who were interested in our diplomatic and commercial relations in China.

In addition to numerous monographs on China, he wrote an exhaustive book on 'Chinese Immigration in its Social and Economical Aspects' (Scribner's, 1881); but the largest number of his literary contributions to diplomatic history will be found in the volumes of the Consular and Diplomatic Reports published by the United States Government. In these volumes will be found a rich store of information concerning our relations with China during the eventful twenty years of Chinese history covered by Mr. Seward's incumbency of his various offices. * * *

Marriage

In 1870 Mr. Seward married Miss Kate Sherman, of Marysville, Cal., 'a lady of accomplishment—being a fine musician, brilliant linguist, and possessed of peculiarly agreeable conversational powers.'" * * *

Interested in Construction of Hudson Tunnels

Some time after his return from China, Mr. Seward was associated with D. C. Haskin in the latter's effort to tunnel the Hudson River from 15th Street, Jersey City, about midway between the present Erie and Lackawanna stations, to a point under Washington Square, New York City. Haskin's idea was to connect with the Pennsylvania, Erie, and Lackawanna railroads near the foot of Bergen Hill, and to bring their traffic to Washington Square, which was at that time considered a convenient point in New York for general distribution. He actually completed 1,800 feet of this tunnel eastward from the Jersey City side under the river, but his company failed in 1882. It may be of interest to know, however, that nine years afterward an English contracting firm undertook the work, but succeeded in completing only about 2,000 feet more. This company in turn failed in 1892. The plan then laid dormant for ten years, when the New York and New Jersey Railroad Company acquired the franchise and property of the old company and undertook the completion of the tunnel. In January, 1905, the Hudson Company was incorporated and eventually took over the Hudson tunnels at that time under construction. The tunnels were opened for traffic from Hoboken, N. J., to Sixth Avenue, Manhattan, February 26, 1908, and on July 19, 1909, those from the Pennsylvania Railroad station in Jersey City to the Hudson Terminal at Cortlandt and Church streets.

Mr. Seward described Haskin's venture at considerable length in a book of some 300 pages, written in coöperation with Mr. S. D. Burr, as a report to the Chamber of Commerce on "Rapid Transit in New York City and in Other Great Cities."

Becomes Interested in Insurance

After a brief association with his friend, Mr. E. E. Clapp, in the general agency of The Fidelity and Casualty Company, Mr. Seward, in 1887, was called to the vice-presidency of The Fidelity and Casualty Company; and on the death of Mr. Richards in 1892, became president.

President of The Fidelity and Casualty Company

He completely identified himself with the business of the company and, with his characteristic zeal and energy, became a potent factor in raising it to a commanding position in the casualty insurance world. He took hold of its affairs at a time when a strong man at the helm was needed. He made his moves carefully and quickly extricated it from every embarrassing situation and placed it upon a firm foundation.

Mr. Seward had the capacity for hard and unremittant labor. The exertion seemed never to tell upon him. He seldom took extended vacations, and could usually be found working at his office throughout the hot summers and during the rest of the year in and out of season.

His Last European Trip

However, in the long run, such unremittant exertion began to tell even upon his iron constitution. Early in the summer of 1909 he began to feel the need of rest and went as far as securing his passage to Europe. But business matters of unusual importance demanding his constant presence at the office, he cancelled the steamship reservation and deferred his trip until the following year.

Those most closely associated with him realized more and more during the rest of the year 1909 and the beginning of 1910 that Mr. Seward would have to take an extended vacation. They used their best efforts to persuade him to go at once; but not seeing his way clear to do so he again deferred his going until the following summer.

Early in June, 1910, he himself realized the absolute necessity of going away for an extended rest, but could not manage to get off until the 21st of July, when he sailed for Europe. In an editorial of the August number of the MONTHLY BULLETIN the following announcement was made: "Our staff will be glad to hear that President Seward sailed for Europe on the 21st of July. His purpose is to get rest and recreation. We are sure that everybody will hope that the trip will prove pleasant and beneficial to him."

Trip Not Permanently Beneficial

Such, however, unfortunately was not destined to be the case. No sooner had the ship sailed out of the harbor than he suffered almost a complete collapse—so much so that it was thought at one time that it would be necessary to return by the next ship.

After landing in Europe, however, he became so much improved that it was thought a sojourn in the Alps would be a great benefit, and thither he went. He undoubtedly got considerable pleasure out of his stay in the mountains, for his descriptions to those of us at the home office after his return were most enthusiastic. From time to time he sent post-card views of the scenes in which he delighted to different members of the home office staff with a paragraph or two descriptive of them in his own handwriting.

Home Coming

From the Alps Mr. Seward travelled through other parts of Europe and finally returned to this country on the 4th of September. Those of us who greeted him upon his return to the office on Tuesday the seventh of that month were shocked to see the inroads that illness had made upon the constitution of the president.

Mr. Seward was at his office rather irregularly until about the first of October, when he almost entirely resigned himself to attending at his house to such business as was absolutely imperative. His secretary visited him almost daily to take such dictation as he thought necessary to give and the home office staff were in almost constant communication with him, either at his house or by messenger, up to within about a fortnight of his death.

Those of us who saw him at his house at 136 West 73rd Street, Manhattan, during these weeks will never forget the interviews held in the library in the front of the house on the second floor. In this room he sat usually upon the sofa in the northwest corner and talked interestingly and instructively upon subjects of business or of personal interest. Thinking that our representatives in the field may be interested in this room in which their former president spent his last days, we have printed on another page of this Memorial a very good photograph, showing the particular corner of the room that he frequented most.

Celebration of His Seventieth Birthday

Notwithstanding his enfeebled condition, Mr. Seward was able on November 8th last to celebrate the seventieth anniversary of his birth with evident comfort and undoubted pleasure. The event was not marked by a formal reception, but a number of friends called to pay their respects and many others sent notes of congratulation.

He received also quantities of most beautiful flowers commemorative of the event; and while appreciative of all of these beautiful tokens of warm regard, his heart glowed with warmth of kindly feeling at the gift of seventy large and beautiful chrysanthemums sent him by the home office stenographers. Touching several of these flowers he gave expression to the following now memorable sentiment:

"Seventy blossoms! each one different from every other one; each complete in itself, and combined, making a group unique in itself. Seventy blossoms, representing seventy years! each year different from every other year; each complete in itself, but combined, representing a life."

He must have felt deeply, upon that occasion, the genuineness of the grateful tributes of respect and regard that were laid at his feet. He must have taken great satisfaction upon contemplating the great corporate structure that he had builded upon the rock foundation of truth and justice. For the institution is but the handiwork of the master builder.

At the beginning of 1910, Mr. Seward circulated broadcast among the agents of the company a New Year's greeting in the form of a little pamphlet entitled "An Outlook and a Promise." In that circular he expressed the hope that the year of his seventieth birthday might be made the occasion of particular felicitation because of the increase in the total business written of ten per cent. over the preceding year. He took great interest in seeing whether the increase would come up to this mark set by him and he had the exquisite pleasure before his death of believing that the result would probably be attained by the end of the year.

In spite of intermittent periods of improvement, Mr. Seward's general physical condition grew slowly but steadily worse after his birthday. Although our optimism (born, as it proved to be, of the object of its eager desire), was at times buoyed up by these fleeting periods of evident improvement, yet even that optimism departed during the week preceding his death. Nevertheless, the end came far more speedily than any of us could have foretold. He suffered an acute relapse on Sunday, November 27th, and on the following day, a little before nine o'clock in the morning, he passed away.

Last Rites

The funeral services were held in the beautiful Madison Square Presbyterian Church, corner Madison Square and 24th Street, Manhattan, at four o'clock in the afternoon of Wednesday, November 30th. Dr. Charles H. Parkhurst delivered the address to an audience that filled the auditorium of the church to its utmost capacity.

There were many distinguished persons present who had come to pay their last respects to the memory of a great man. There were representatives from the Chamber of Commerce of New York, from the Board of Directors of The Fidelity and Casualty Company, from the Board of Trustees of Union College, from the New York Alumni Association of Union College, from the Sons of the Revolution, and from The Board of Casualty and Surety Underwriters, The International Association of Accident Underwriters, and The Detroit Conference.

The services in the church were very simple, consisting, in addition to an address of Dr. Parkhurst, of music by the church choir, and a prayer by Rev. Andrew V. V. Raymond, D.D., formerly president of Union College. The pulpit and chancel were beautifully decorated with appropriate flowers and plants.

Interment was made privately at Woodlawn Cemetery, Thursday, December 1st—only members of the family and a few intimate friends being present. Rev. George Alexander, D.D., for years an intimate friend of Mr. Seward, conducted the services at the grave.

In addition to his widow, Mrs. Kate Sherman Seward, Mr. Seward leaves four children to mourn his loss—Mrs. Maurice Kaufman, Mr. George O. Seward, Miss Anne L. Seward, and Miss Emma Seward.

1. Mr. Seward (about 1865)
2. Mr. Seward (about 1875)
3. Mr. Seward (about 1877)
4. Mr. Seward (about 1887)
5. Mr. Seward (about 1898)
6. Mr. Seward (about 1905)
7. Mr. Seward's favorite photograph (about 1902)

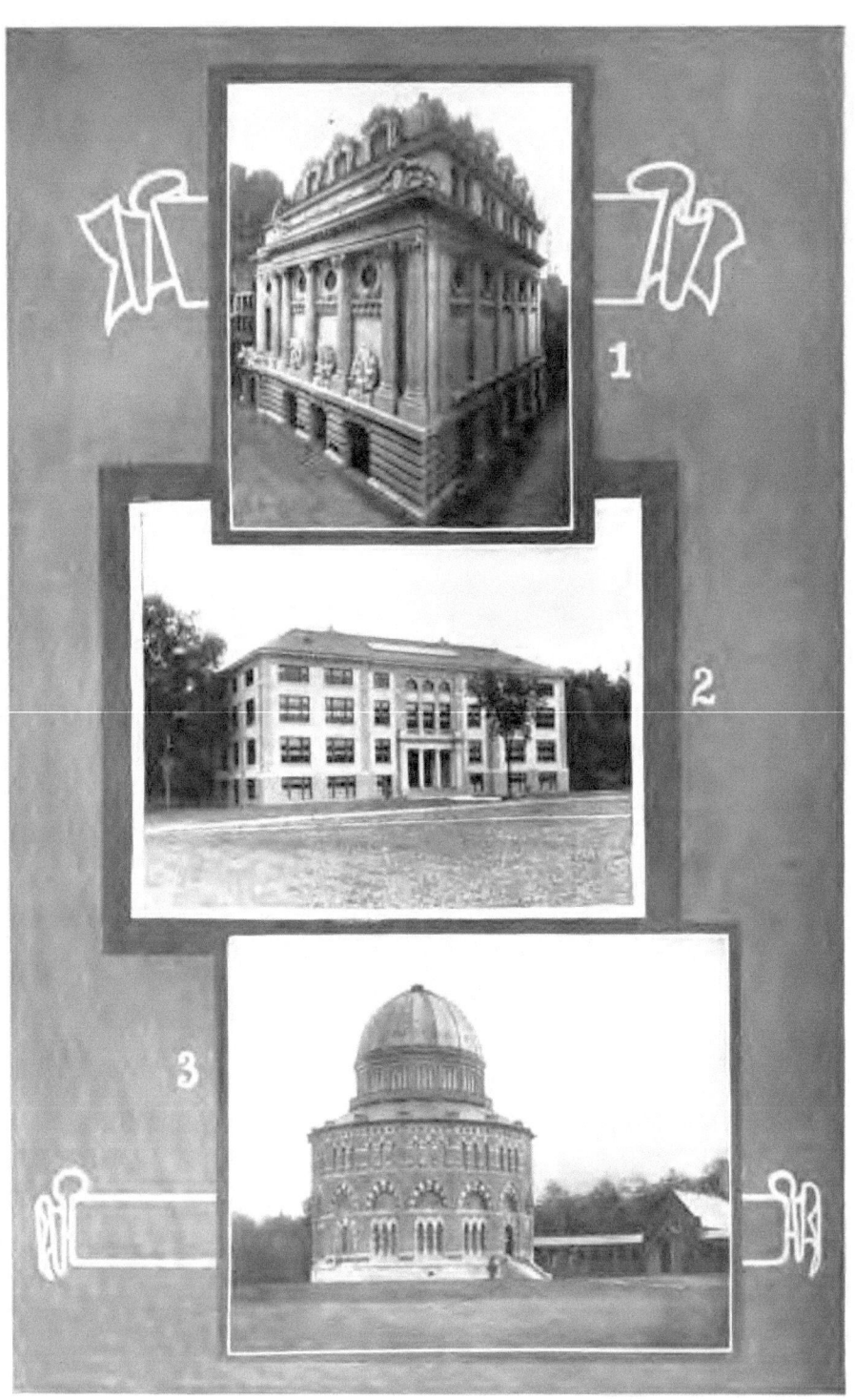

1. New York Chamber of Commerce Building
2. Engineering Building at Union College, Schenectady, N. Y.
3. Library Building at Union College, Schenectady, N. Y.

MR. SEWARD'S WORK FOR UNION COLLEGE

Notwithstanding Mr. Seward's close attention to all the numerous details of the business of a great corporation, he nevertheless found ample time to devote his tremendous energies to outside interests that had claims upon him for one reason or another. Of all these outside activities probably there were none that gave him more genuine pleasure than those devoted to the interests of Union College at Schenectady, New York, his *alma mater*.

He entered that college when not quite fifteen years of age, but was obliged to leave before the end of the term to assume the direction of his family's landed estate. The college conferred upon him, however, in 1904, the honorary degree of LL.D.—having several years before made him a member of the Board of Trustees.

It is unnecessary to record that these honors were a source of great pleasure and satisfaction to him, owing to the fact that Union was, so to speak, the college of his family; for it was there that his great uncle, William Henry Seward, Secretary of State under Lincoln, was educated; likewise his brother, Rev. Samuel S. Seward, his cousin Frederick W. Seward, son of the Secretary, and other relatives.

Mr. Seward at the very start took a prominent position in the direction of the affairs of the college, and so great were the material results of his activities on its behalf that, when he reluctantly resigned his position in the Board of Trustees at the Commencement in 1910 on account of failing health, his retirement was regarded by all interested in the affairs of the college as a misfortune. None regretted his action, however, more than he.

Mr. Seward was chairman of the committee of the Board of Trustees in charge of grounds and buildings. In this capacity he attended to all of the numerous executive details involved in the construction of the beautiful Engineering Building, a picture of which we show on another page. He was active in the reconstruction of the by-laws of the Board, and was largely instrumental in having introduced in the proceedings of that organization up-to-date businesslike methods.

Mr. Seward's name, however, is likewise identified closely with the successful efforts to secure from Andrew Carnegie funds sufficient to reconstruct the Potter Memorial Building for modern library purposes. Mr. Seward went with a few other gentlemen to Mr. Carnegie's house and personally urged upon him the necessities of the college and the wisdom of making a considerable gift in money. As a result of these efforts, Mr. Carnegie contributed a large sum of money which made possible the present Library Building. We show a picture of this building also.

Of Mr. Seward's activities on behalf of Union College, President Charles Alexander Richmond of that institution, writes as follows:

"The name of Seward is closely connected with Union College, and the memory of the Sewards is one of its valued inheritances. Mr. George F. Seward devoted a very appreciable portion of his time to the interests of his *alma mater* and to this service he brought the good judgment and the conscientious attention to detail which characterized all his work. He was never too busy with his own affairs to attend to college matters. As a trustee of the college and for years as the chairman of the committee in charge of grounds and buildings, he rendered services which will long be remembered. He was mainly instrumental in securing funds for the completion of the Library Building and also for the new Engineering Building—the gift of Mr. Carnegie.

Union College has lost a warm friend and a devoted son in his death.

My personal sense of loss is deep and sincere."

MR. SEWARD'S WORK IN THE CHAMBER OF COMMERCE

Among the other outside interests that engrossed a large part of Mr. Seward's time, not devoted to the interests of his company, was his work on behalf of the public good in the Chamber of Commerce of the State of New York. His interest in this institution was almost a passion with him, and upon whatever committee he found himself placed, he went to work with that energy and enthusiasm that was so characteristic of him in every obligation that he assumed. He did not become a member of the Chamber until 1897, "but almost from the beginning," says the *Monthly Bulletin* published by that institution, "he took a high place in its deliberations."

"His work in the insurance field had led him to study questions of taxation, and becoming Chairman of the Chamber's Committee on State and Municipal Taxation he presented during the past ten years a series of reports on taxation which it is no exaggeration to say were masterpieces of research and analysis. His work in influencing wise legislation in regard to taxation was most important and involved on his part a vast amount of labor.

"Last May the Chamber, as a recognition of his services, promoted him to the Chairmanship of the Executive Committee. No sketch of Mr. Seward's career in this Chamber would be complete without reference to his preparation in 1905-6 of the 'History of Rapid Transit in New York and Other Cities,' which was published by the Chamber and was and still is an authoritative publication on this subject. For this work he received the thanks of the Chamber. In moving these thanks Mr. Hepburn, in March, 1906, spoke of Mr. Seward's great ability and broad and varied experience and declared that there could be no higher evidence of his devotion to the Chamber than his preparation of this magnificent book."

From his position as Chairman of the Executive Committee, had his health not failed him, he would undoubtedly have been promoted in due course to the presidency of the Chamber, the former office, according to custom and tradition, being considered in direct line of succession to the latter highly honorable and influential position.

In addition to the chairmanship of the Executive Committee, the Chamber had likewise conferred upon him the honor of a vice-presidency for an official term.

Upon his return from Europe, Mr. Seward announced at the September meeting of the Executive Committee of the Chamber that he might have to retire from his activities, much as he would regret doing so. Later, however, upon the improvement of his health he resumed for the time his customary round of duties. It was then, quoting from the Chamber's *Monthly Bulletin* again, "beautiful to witness the affection with which he was welcomed back by his associates in his business, and the pride which he exhibited in their abilities and zeal."

One of the keenest pleasures, we believe, that came into Mr. Seward's full life upon assuming his high offices in the Chamber, was the fact that he had made a notable conquest of the confidence and esteem of that great body, which is said to have protested against his assumption of the duties of Consul at Shanghai in 1861, urging as a reason that he was too youthful and inexperienced.

Let us quote from the proceedings of the Chamber the impressive tributes that were paid to Mr. Seward's memory at the regular meeting, Thursday, December 1, 1910:

"THE PRESIDENT [A. Barton Hepburn].—Gentlemen, it is my very sad duty to announce officially the death of one of the more prominent members of this Chamber, the Chairman of your Executive Committee, Mr. George F. Seward. He was an educated, cultivated gentleman, belonging to one of our historic families. He early entered public life in the diplomatic service, and for many years represented us in the Orient in a most painstaking and successful manner. He died full of years and full of honors, leaving behind a record and a memory of which his family and his fellow citizens may well be proud.

"ANTON A. RAVEN.—Mr. President, it is fitting that we should pay suitable respect to the memory of Mr. Seward. I move, therefore, that this Chamber now adjourn, but before the adjournment I wish to make a few remarks regarding Mr. Seward. Most of the gentlemen of this Chamber knew him. He was no ordinary man: he was a man of great worth, possessing qualities which attracted friends. He was always ready to assist those who were closely associated with him in the company of which he was the honored president. No one knew him but to love him.

To have understood Mr. Seward thoroughly was to appreciate his high character, a character that this Chamber may well be proud of as representing one of its vice-presidents. I move, therefore, that suitable expression of our appreciation of his character be placed on our records. It certainly will be an inspiration to others to pursue the path that he pursued.

"ALEXANDER E. ORR.—Mr. President, I desire to second the motion made by Mr. Raven. I am also one of those deeply grieved over the death of George F. Seward, and thoroughly appreciate the loss we all have sustained. I feel I am justified in giving expression to the warm sympathy I have with each member of the Chamber over that sad event.

"I came to know Mr. Seward after his return from China as his country's representative, and when he entered into relationship with the insurance company with which for very many years he has been connected as its respected and successful president.

"I presume we are all aware of the deep interest he took in advancing the business conditions of this city and state, indeed I should say of the whole United States, through the instrumentality of this Chamber, which, strictly interpreted, is entitled to recognition as the commercial guardian of this great country of ours. His activity and courage in this direction were untiring, and were graciously recognized by you in electing him to the honorable position of Chairman of the Executive Committee, which I know added greatly to his happiness in his later years.

"Although a strict disciplinarian in the management of the business of his adoption, in which he became a past master, he possessed the respect and regard of his junior officers and employees, and the abiding confidence and friendship of the members of his board of directors, and of very many others in similar business relations, with whom he came in almost daily contact, and among whom he became a recognized leader.

"I do not think that you wish me to accentuate what has been so well said by the President and Mr. Raven. I believe it will be more in keeping with your wishes if I simply second the motion now before the Chamber, that we adjourn as a mark of respect to the memory of our late friend and fellow member, and that we adopt this by a rising vote.

"The motion was unanimously adopted, by all standing in reverent silence."

A fine half-tone of Mr. Seward is printed in the January, 1911, issue of the *Monthly Bulletin* of the Chamber—the issue from which we have made the above quotations. We print on another page a picture of the Chamber of Commerce building, 65 Liberty Street, Manhattan.

MR. SEWARD'S LITERARY WORK

In spite of his activities in many directions and the tremendous energy and unquestioned conscientiousness that he displayed in them, Mr. Seward nevertheless found time to devote a considerable part of his intellectual endowments to literary pursuits. He was a man of broad and deep reading, of scholarly habits and attainments, and of a refined literary taste.

As an illustration of the breadth of his interests as a scholar, we might cite the fact that at one time he would be reading works upon history, then works upon economics and politics, and so on—even to scientific treatises upon the geology of his native state.

Mr. Seward's scholarly attainments, however, were exemplified particularly in the books and monographs that his fertile mind and flexible intellect made it possible for him to produce. We have referred in other connections to his book on "Chinese Immigration in its Social and Economical Aspects," printed by Charles Scribner's Sons in 1881. This is a classical work of four hundred twenty-one pages, and is still accepted as an authority upon the subjects with which it deals. As a concrete illustration of this statement, the writer of these memorials may point to the fact that some years ago, when he was called upon to act as judge of an interclass debate at Vassar College upon the subject "Should the Chinese be excluded from the United States," he found that the whole case of the negative side of the question was established upon Mr. Seward's book, and that his name was quoted frequently as a conclusive authority upon the points made.

Mr. Seward embodied in this book the observations and conclusions of his whole Oriental experience, and brought to bear the full power of his intellectual force upon the issues then prominent.

We have likewise referred to his preparation in 1905-6 of the "History of Rapid Transit in New York and Other Cities," which was published by the Chamber of Commerce in a handsome volume of three hundred pages, and which is still an authoritative publication on that subject.

We have referred, likewise, to his series of reports on taxation as chairman of the Chamber's Committee on State and Municipal Taxation; and it is no exaggeration to say that they were masterpieces of research and analysis.

In addition to these literary works of wider interest, Mr. Seward wrote numerous monographs, brochures, and briefs dealing with insurance interests in general, casualty insurance interests in particular, and miscellaneous oriental subjects. Among those printed might be mentioned the following which are of particular importance: "The State and Casualty Insurance," "Life Insurance Investments," "The Right to Contract *versus* Legislation to Make Standard Policy Provisions," "Withdrawal of License as Penalty for Violation of State Insurance Laws," "Insurance is Commerce," "Federal Supervision of Insurance," "Justice to China," "How to Avoid War," "The Philippine Question Again," "The United States and China," "The Russian-Japanese War," and "Philippine Autonomy."

In all of Mr. Seward's literary productions, the most important characteristic features are lucidity of style, logical analysis, orderly development, and conciseness of expression.

One always marvelled, when watching Mr. Seward write a paper or outline a brief, at the remarkable facility with which he put down abstruse ideas rapidly and with a logical orderliness. So rapidly could he express his ideas in writing that one was impelled to believe it was the result largely of native ability. No doubt it was, to a very large extent, although he always combated that idea. He claimed that he acquired the habit during his consular and diplomatic service by always analyzing carefully his propositions, putting them down in the proper logical order, and then rather laboriously building up the word-superstructure. He held, too, that this, in the case of most people, was the tribute they had to pay for the possession of a facile pen and lucid style.

Mr. Seward spoke as he wrote, measuring every word and giving to it the proper thought value. He maintained the proposition, furthermore, which we believe must be limited by many qualifications, that whoever could think straight, could likewise write clearly; and *vice versa*, that whoever wrote lucidly, thought clearly.

MONTHLY BULLETIN

We should not consider complete a sketch of Mr. Seward's activities that did not include at least a brief mention of his work on the company's paper, the MONTHLY BULLETIN.

The MONTHLY BULLETIN was founded by him in 1895, and the first number was issued in November of that year. It is now in its 16th volume, and during all these years the paper has not failed to greet the agency force of the company once a month.

In his editorial "Salutatory" in the first number, Mr. Seward announced certain fundamental principles that he would adhere to in editing the paper. It was to be "for the information of the company's agents," but the publication was not to be treated as confidential; "for," wrote he, "we think that our methods are such that we could admit the public to the knowledge of them with advantage to ourselves." He announced as the Fidelity and Casualty creed "efficient management, reasonable rates, honorable dealing," and stated that this creed "well-observed would conduce to our welfare in the future as it has in the past."

He announced, furthermore, that "we will not indulge in random criticisms of competitors." The paragraph announcing this principle is so characteristic that we cannot refrain from quoting it in full:

> We will not indulge in random criticisms of competitors. Comparisons are odious in well-regulated society. Business, however, involves many comparisons. Some goods are good and some are not and the good salesman should know the one from the other if he is to be useful in his day and generation. But there is no reason why a salesman should go outside of his proper avocation in this respect. Courtesy to competitors is an unvarying rule of our office. We do not promise, however, to refrain from right criticism when things are done by competitors which are in wanton violation of sound insurance rules. We hope there will be very little occasion for this kind of criticism. It is much pleasanter to attend to our own business than to that of other people. It is, indeed, only when wrong courses touch our interests that we shall feel called upon to talk in that direction.

The reader can judge for himself how exactly these principles have been lived up to through all subsequent issues of the BULLETIN; for not only did Mr. Seward dictate absolutely its policy, but he edited conscientiously every paragraph printed in it and wrote nearly all of the editorials—at least up to the last few years.

It is fitting, therefore, that the MONTHLY BULLETIN, Mr. Seward's creation and constant interest, the mouthpiece through which he spoke, not only to the agency force but likewise to the insurance world at large, should attempt to do him honor.

MR. SEWARD'S WORK ON BEHALF OF INSURANCE ASSOCIATIONS

It was natural that Mr. Seward should take a prominent part in the deliberations of the various casualty insurance associations by reason of his great ability and the prominence of his company.

He rendered incalculable service in connection with the Liability Conference of which he was one of the founders and to the end a stanch and loyal supporter. To the work of that body, more than to any other cause, is due, we believe, the fact that the liability business in this country has been placed upon a sound and enduring basis.

In his work in the Conference, he stood always for the ascertainment of rates—on scientific principles. He stood stanchly for sound underwriting and for whatever made for the improvement of the business.

He was constantly concerned regarding the prevention of accidents, and as a concrete illustration of his interest in eliminating unnecessary hazards to the lives and limbs of employees, we point with pardonable pride to the magnificent work compiled in this office by Mr. Frank E. Law and Mr. William Newell, entitled "The Prevention of Industrial Accidents." Many thousands of this book were distributed among employers throughout this country. In announcing the completion of volume I of this work, Mr. Seward wrote editorially in the November, 1909, BULLETIN as follows:

> A book with the above title, belonging to a series for which we have been accumulating data for three years, is in the press and will be issued in a few days. We believe it to be the first attempt that has been made in this country to gather together in a systematic treatise what has been settled by experience with regard to the prevention of industrial accidents. It is the work of men in this office who know the subject from the practical side—as engineers and underwriters. In preparing it they have had the benefit of all our own data, and they have made thoroughgoing studies in other directions. This pamphlet deals with the hazards common to all industries. The supplementary pamphlets of the series to be issued later will deal with the hazards peculiar to specific industries.
>
> If our conclusion is right that sixty per cent. of all industrial accidents may be prevented, and if this book clearly describes how they may be prevented, the work we have done should be valuable not only to employers, but to our company as an insurer and to other companies engaged in liability insurance.
>
> It has always been to us a source of keen satisfaction that the work of our office runs so largely on lines beneficial to the public. How many lives have been saved by the work of our inspectors, notably of steam boilers and of elevators, cannot be told, but the number must have been large. And while the inspection of liability risks has never been possible for us or for any other company in the same measure as that of boilers or elevators our work in that direction has been considerable, and here again we may be credited with having saved lives.

Closely allied with his work in the Conference, was Mr. Seward's work in the Liability Association. Here, too, he was an important factor for the betterment of fundamental conditions in the liability business.

Mr. Seward was likewise one of the organizers of The Board of Casualty and Surety Underwriters—being a member of the "Committee of Ten" appointed at the first meeting, September 27, 1904, upon whose report the Board was organized on December 9th following, Hotel Astor, New York City.

Mr. Seward was elected Chairman of the Executive Committee right from the start and held that office up to the day of his death. In this position he had an opportunity of doing work of lasting benefit to casualty and surety interests.

He maintained at no expense to the Board an effective bureau for reporting and investigating insurance measures introduced in the various state legislatures; and he combated obnoxious measures in effective briefs submitted to the different state insurance committees.

With the exception of the last annual meeting of the Board, when he was ill, he seldom ever absented himself from the council chambers of that organization; and one marvelled that he found time and energy to bear the heavy burdens placed upon him by his interest in the work.

Though Mr. Seward was never personally active in the councils of The International Association of Accident Underwriters, yet he was a firm supporter of that organization, and always saw to it that The Fidelity and Casualty Company was represented at its annual meetings.

Mr. Seward's co-operation was had, likewise, in other insurance organizations, among which we might name the Burglary Association, the Plate Glass Association, and the Excise Reinsurance Association.

These activities of Mr. Seward in casualty and surety organizations, conclusively prove that he was willing and eager to co-operate with his competitors when such co-operation promised a betterment of business conditions. In fact, considerable credit is due him, through his co-operation with other companies, for the relatively high moral standards that now prevail for the most part in the business.

MEMORIALS OF ORGANIZATIONS IN WHICH MR. SEWARD WAS INTERESTED

After the death of Mr. Seward, the organizations with which he was most closely allied held meetings at which formal memorials were drawn up and sent to the members of the family. Those drafted by the Board of Directors of The Fidelity and Casualty Company, the managers and general agents of the company, and the home office staff, were beautifully engrossed in Old English lettering on vellum and artistically bound in leather, or mounted in frames.

The first two pages of the Board's memorial, we reproduce in half-tone on the first pages of this issue of the BULLETIN. This memorial is beautifully lettered in black, gold, and purple upon heavy vellum and is bound in olive green leather stamped with a narrow band of gold—making a beautiful and appropriate work of artistic value.

The memorial of the home office staff is engrossed in script lettering upon vellum and bound in black leather; and that of the managers and general agents of the company is wrought similarly but is set in a frame. Each of these memorials has the autograph of the appropriate persons.

We reproduce herewith all of these memorials that have come to our hands.

Minute of the Board of Directors

At a special meeting of the Board of Directors of the Fidelity and Casualty Company, held December 7, 1910, the following minute was adopted:

"In the Providence of God, our president, George F. Seward, has been taken from our midst, after twenty-three years of service with the company; for the first six years as vice-president and for the last seventeen years as president thereof.

"During his term of service the company has prospered remarkably, its multiplied strength bearing eloquent testimony to the skill and fidelity of its management, in which Mr. Seward, as president, occupied the foremost place. Before his connection with the company, he had served the Government of the United States in its consular and diplomatic services in responsible positions and brought to the company the benefits derived from such experience and training; something unusual for an insurance company to obtain. He acquired such a knowledge of the business we transact as to make him an acknowledged expert and leader in it. With his remarkable capacity he was not contented to confine his interest wholly to this company, but became a valued and conspicuous member of the New York Chamber of Commerce, besides taking a good citizen's interest in matters pertaining to the public welfare.

"There are but three or four left who were directors when Mr. Seward came, but all have served long enough with him, as fellow director and chief officer, to know that in his death they have sustained a personal loss. Always ready to impart information about the affairs of the company to the directors, he made the doing of this so interesting and agreeable as often to keep around him, even after meetings of the directors were ended, a group that eagerly drank in what he had to tell. It seems almost needless to say that his cheerful and dignified presence will be greatly missed.

"We extend our sincere condolences to his bereaved family and direct that a copy of this minute be sent to them and also that it be recorded in our book of minutes and given to the press."

Resolutions of the Managers and General Agents of The Fidelity and Casualty Company

At a meeting of the managers and general agents of The Fidelity and Casualty Company from all parts of the country, held at 66 Pine Street, New York City, at 12 o'clock noon on Friday, December 2, 1910, the following resolutions were adopted:

"WHEREAS, our late president, George Frederick Seward, has been called to rest in the height of his glorious career, when he had just attained the three score years and ten of life; and

"WHEREAS, his death is not only a great grief to his well-loved family and friends, but an irreparable loss to all his associates in business, to the officials, managers, agents, and employees of the great company he built up, to the business of insurance in general, and to the whole nation which he served so long and so ably, both in public and private life.

"Now Therefore Be it

"RESOLVED, That the managers and general agents, all of whom knew and loved him, many of whom had served with him during their whole business careers, hereby extend to the widow and family of the late President Seward, and to the directors and officers of the company, our deepest sympathies in their bereavement, and in the loss they have suffered.

"MR. SEWARD was a man of unusual attainments and breadth of mind, who early became nobly conspicuous among men. His achievements are written in the annals of the nation, are perpetuated in the great company which stands as a monument to his rare abilities, and are forever engraved in the lasting memories of those who shared in his work.

"An intellectual giant, a born statesman, with a genius for administration, he filled to the full his diverse functions of diplomat, business man, and citizen, and every post he ever held was magnified by his occupancy.

"Of brilliant mind, of charming personality, of amiable and lovable character, deliberate of thought, energetic of action, it was a privilege to know him; his judgment was keen, his motives magnanimous, and his mind pointed irresistibly to the true and right.

"Be it Further

"RESOLVED, that a copy of these Resolutions be presented to his family and to the Board of Directors of The Fidelity and Casualty Company."

Resolutions of the Home Office Staff of The Fidelity and Casualty Company

At a meeting of the officers, superintendents and assistant superintendents of The Fidelity and Casualty Company of New York on December 28, 1910, the following resolutions were unanimously adopted:

"BE IT RESOLVED, That we, the associates of the late George F. Seward in his daily business life, place on record our admiration of his material achievements as evidenced in the upbuilding and guidance of the vast business with which he has so long been identified, our affection for him as inspired by his just and kindly attitude toward all, and our high esteem of his character in general as tested by years of close intimacy. His name will ever be held in the deepest veneration by us and by the other members of our staff.

"BE IT ALSO RESOLVED, That these minutes be engrossed and forwarded to Mrs. Seward with the assurance of our affectionate sympathy for herself and children in their loss."

Resolutions of The Board of Casualty and Surety Underwriters

At a special meeting of The Board of Casualty and Surety Underwriters, held in the City of New York on the twenty-ninth day of November, nineteen hundred and ten, the following preamble and resolutions were unanimously adopted:

"WHEREAS, Divine Providence has, in His infinite wisdom, removed from his earthly labors our late associate, George F. Seward, it is

"RESOLVED, That by his death the world of casualty insurance has lost one of its most learned members, wisest counselors and efficient co-workers, and that each member of this board has forever been deprived of a personal friend.

"BE IT FURTHER RESOLVED, That this Board extend to the family of our departed friend our deep sympathy in this the hour of their bereavement, and to the officers and staff of The Fidelity and Casualty Company, which Mr. Seward, as president, brought into such a commanding position through his industry, intelligence, and skill, expressions of our sincere sorrow for their loss.

"Mr. Seward was a man of exceeding energy, unusual mental attainment, and he possessed personal qualities which closely bound to him all those whose privilege it was to enjoy his friendship.

"BE IT FURTHER RESOLVED, That this preamble and these resolutions be spread upon the minutes of this Board.

Resolutions of the Liability Insurance Association

At a meeting of the Liability Insurance Association, held November 29, 1910, the following resolutions were adopted:

"WHEREAS, The Liability Insurance Association has learned with profound regret of the death of George F. Seward, president of The Fidelity and Casualty Company of New York, be it

"RESOLVED, That this association tenders its deep sympathy to the members of his family, and to the directors and officers of the company, in his untimely death.

"It is the sense of this association that the insurance world at large has lost one of its most eminent and respected representatives through the death of Mr. Seward, and that the casualty insurance companies particularly will find it difficult to replace him who has done so much to promote and maintain the highest standard in the business of casualty insurance; that the members of the association attend Mr. Seward's funeral, and pay him this last tribute of respect.

"BE IT FURTHER RESOLVED, That this resolution be spread upon the minutes of the association, and that a copy, suitably engrossed, be presented to his family."

Resolutions of the General Committee, Excise Reinsurance Association

At the third meeting of the General Committee of the Excise Reinsurance Association, held at the offices of The Fidelity and Casualty Company, New York City, December 17, 1910, the following resolutions were unanimously adopted, and the secretary was instructed to have them engrossed and sent to the widow of the deceased:

"RESOLVED, that we record with profound sorrow the death of our esteemed friend and chairman, Mr. George F. Seward, whose interest in the affairs of the Excise Reinsurance Association, from its inception some years ago until his death recently occurring, was of inestimable value to the member companies and to their representatives on the various committees. Mr. Seward's untiring zeal on behalf of the Association, his keen foresight and unusual ability to measure and weigh every condition presenting itself for consideration, and, finally, his singleness of purpose in the perpetuation of the Association, regardless of disadvantages to his own company, created the most implicit confidence in him by all of the members and their representatives, and now accentuate in the hearts and minds of all the loss that has come to them in his taking away.

"AND BE IT RESOLVED, that we express our heartfelt sympathy for the members of his family.

"AND BE IT FURTHER RESOLVED, that these resolutions be spread upon the records of the Association, and a copy thereof sent to his family."

SOCIETIES AND DECORATIONS

During his long career as a diplomat and business man, Mr. Seward had many honors conferred upon him, and held membership in a number of learned and scientific organizations.

Of all of the honors conferred upon him, he probably esteemed most highly the decoration of the Order of Annam, and that of Knight Commander of Danebrog.

He was admitted to the Order of Annam by the French Republic for his instrumentality in quelling with a strong hand a dangerous riot at Shanghai.

He was created a Knight Commander of Danebrog—the Grand Cross of the Order being awarded him—by the King of Denmark, for his successful conclusion in 1874 of the negotiations with the Chinese authorities, giving admission and security to a system of telegraphs and cables established by a Danish company along the coast of China.

Mr. Seward was a member of the American Geographical Society, American Academy of Political and Social Science, New England Society of Orange, N. J., Historical Society of Orange, N. J., American Institute of Civics, American Electrochemical Society, American Peace Society, Civil Service Reform Association, National Municipal League, Merchants' Association of New York, Sons of the Revolution, and Union College Alumni Association of New York.

He was, likewise, a trustee of Union College, a governor of Union University, president of the Virginia Electrolytic Company, Tin Products Company, vice-president of the Virginia Laboratory Company, and vice-president and chairman of the Executive Committee of the New York Chamber of Commerce.

He was also a member of a number of clubs, including the Authors', Lawyers', Reform, and Patria.

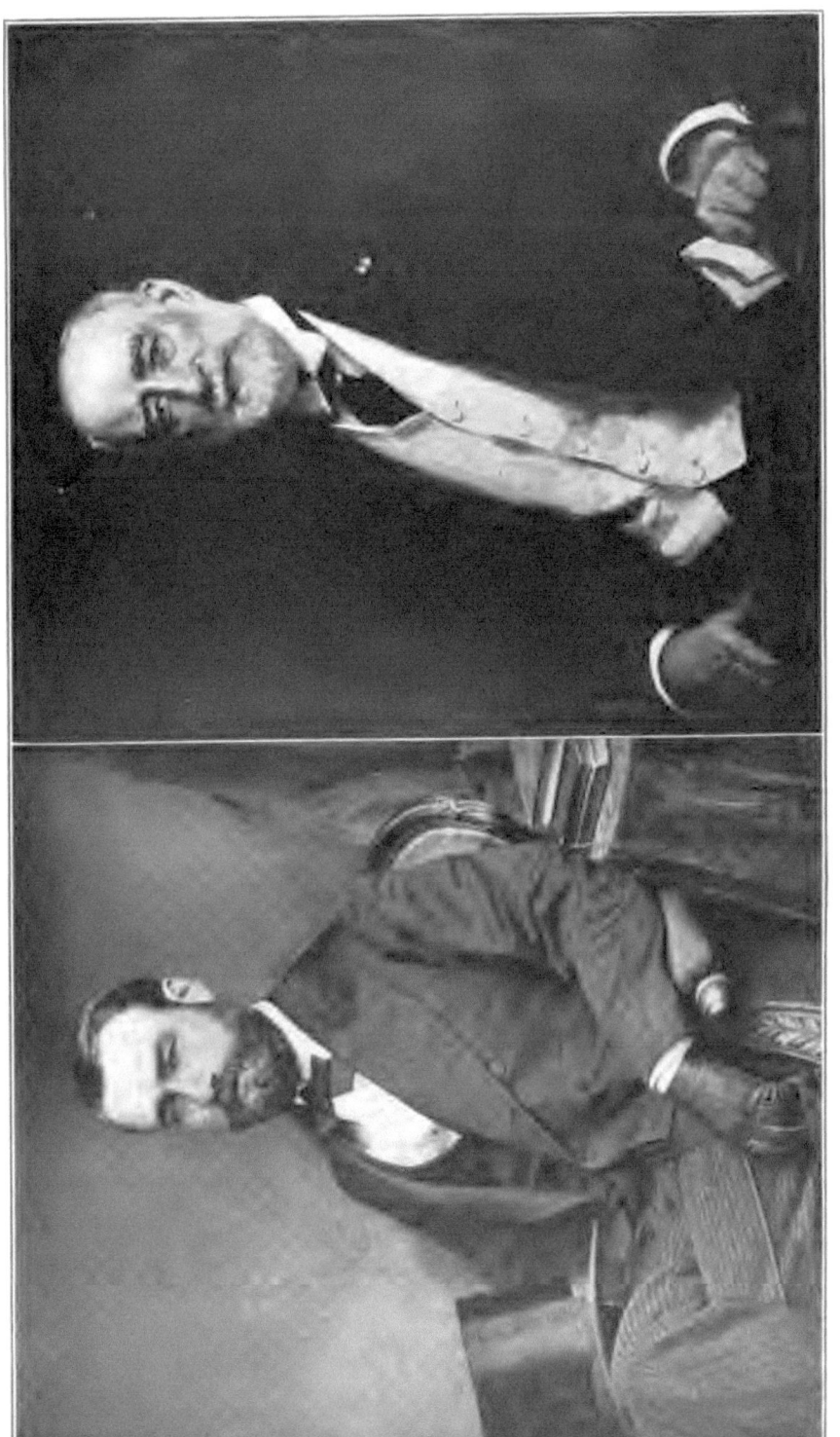

Mr. Seward (about 1865)

Reproduced from a recent Painting by Irving R. Wiles

Photograph of Mr. Seward (June, 1906) at his desk, 97 Cedar Street

PERSONAL TRIBUTES TO MR. SEWARD'S CHARACTER AND ABILITY

We print herewith a group of personal tributes to Mr. Seward's character and ability from his contemporaries in the insurance business who knew him best.

An "Appreciation" by Edson S. Lott

Edson S. Lott, president of the United States Casualty Company, New York City, paid a tribute to Mr. Seward's character and ability in *Assurance*, May, 1909, which we quote in part as follows:

I am asked to write "an appreciation" of George Frederick Seward. It's a big job. Bigger than many people in the insurance business think. I'm glad to do it, but I wish I could borrow, while doing it, John T. Stone's pen—or Charles D. Lakey's. In the first place, what is *an appreciation?* The dictionary defines *appreciation* as

"* * * True or adequate apprehension or estimate, as of qualities, merit, value, etc.* * * Susceptibility or sensitiveness to delicate distinctions; keen perception as to points not obvious. * * *"

Now, after the dictionary has been consulted and one has ascertained what is expected of him when writing an appreciation of any one, and when he starts in on the job in connection with the name of George F. Seward, he realizes that the job is a big one. At least, I do.

Here is a man capable of creditably filling the position of Secretary of State—indeed, a man well equipped—possessing the necessary natural and acquired all-around ability and experience to make a good President of this glorious country * *; and *I* am asked to write *an appreciation* of him. Mind you, I must estimate truly and adequately his qualities, merits, and value; I must be capable of making delicate distinctions in describing his virtues and his faults; I must have keen perception that I may discover points not obvious—for the dictionary says so—and that's what I want to do. I want to describe him as *I* see him—excellences and faults. This is not a eulogy.

Before the above was written, the data concerning Mr. Seward had been gathered. I dare say that there are those engaged in the business of casualty insurance—and consider themselves well informed—who believe that Mr. Seward was never employed in any other work than that of insurance, except as a side issue or diversion—that he began his life's work in the world of insurance and grew up with it. If any of those read this article they will realize how wrong they were, and how right I am when I claim that it is a big job to write an appreciation of a man as big as Mr. Seward.

Here's the record as I find it; but before getting down to the real details I would like to inform my readers that it is proper to write "Hon." before and "LL.D." after the name of George Frederick Seward, a distinction which he alone of all casualty insurance underwriters enjoys.

Those who think that Mr. Seward has spent a lifetime in insurance work, those who think that he grew up with the business, are requested to note that I've used quite a bit of newspaper space in writing about his career, without even mentioning his entrance into the realm of insurance. That was in 1887—some twenty-odd years ago—when he was elected vice-president of the then struggling Fidelity & Casualty Company. In 1892 he succeeded to the presidency. The company was still struggling. But it doesn't struggle these days. It just glides. The dictionary says of *glide:*

"To move along with ease; flow without violence; pass rapidly, smoothly, and with little apparent effort."

Yes, the "F & C" *glides* now-a-days.

But I can't say that Mr. Seward glides in his work, although he probably waltzes well; he's certainly a lover of music. No, Mr. Seward does not glide in his work. He is too painstaking, too thorough, too sure. When he's working (which is nearly always) he doesn't glide, he grinds—grinds exceeding fine. Whatever Mr. Seward does, he does thoroughly. When he starts out to inform himself on any subject, he does not take anything for granted—he doesn't assume a part and guess at the rest. He doesn't assume anything or guess at anything. He forms his conclusions after informing himself. He isn't always right. Bless you, no. He sometimes disagrees with me. I always regret these rare occasions, for I don't enjoy arguing with him any more than with James V. Barry. And yet I don't know a man who more quickly or more gracefully yields when he is convinced that he is wrong—excepting always those infrequent occasions when he "gets his dander up"—those times when nothing but the grace of God would change his mind. And when he's thoroughly aroused, what a fighter he is! Ordinarily Mr. Seward speaks slowly and softly, and not very distinctly. But when he's angered his words fall atop of each other, each one the best that could be used to express his thoughts, not a waste one among the lot, while his enunciation is exact, clear-cut, and distinct. It's a good scheme for the man who picks a quarrel with George F. Seward to have both the facts and justice on his side. And then he's not sure to win. Sometimes when I've seen Mr. Seward under the stress of vigorous debate I've thought that he imagined he was back in China and still "judge, jury, and executioner." And then he has been known to leave off his own work and go to the office of a small competitor personally to offer an apology for what he considered lack of courtesy on the part of his office to that competitor. And he always gives liberally of his sympathy, his money, and his time in behalf of a sick or unfortunate employee, and not a man in the business is quicker to extend a helping hand to a fair competitor.

Around the council table with other casualty

executives Mr. Seward is usually the last man to express his opinion, and then I do not believe he ever once gave voice to a sentiment simply because it appeared to be the consensus of opinion of those who had spoken. And neither is it his habit to disagree through perverseness. He always says what he thinks, and he usually advances convincing reasons in support of his position. In any event his courage to state his own views, irrespective of the views of the masses, never forsakes him. Mr. Seward is a most lucid and forceful debater. I have seen him cause a roomful of men to change their minds and their votes through listening to his presentation of his opinion. He is not as graceful a talker as Mr. Dunham, not as witty as Captain Masters, not as adroit as Mr. Stone, not as pithy as Mr. Appleton, but he is more persuasive than any one of these masters of the English language.

* * * * * I cannot imagine a more convincing proof of the excellence of his general judgment than the all-conquering field force that carries the insignia of the Fidelity & Casualty, nor do I know of a better place of observation than the camp of a competitor—any competitor. In this connection it occurs to me that Mr. Seward was the first man in the business to make a success of having the company's field work conducted by resident managers, and many a company's executive has since made a dismal failure trying to imitate his plan of campaign in the field. Although there are occasions when I differ with Mr. Seward in his estimate of men, yet I ascribe these differences to the fact that he is too big in every way to take cognizance of the frailties of a less gifted or less honorable associate.

While Mr. Seward willingly extends help to all worthy competitors, he wants to do it in his own way—which is most natural, I suppose. He has for many years tried consistently and persistently to improve conditions in liability lines. He has expended time and money—and both intelligently—for the betterment of this line of insurance; and I am sure that the burdens all liability insurance men are carrying are not as heavy as they would be had not Mr. Seward turned the tide somewhat, at least.

But when we come to accident and health business we look in vain for evidences of material co-operation from Mr. Seward. He will work side by side with any man in the business at any time for improved conditions in liability lines, while he never has any time to devote to the betterment of accident or health lines, if we except the work he is now doing in connection with standard policy provisions.

All in all, the business of casualty insurance is better because George F. Seward has been engaged in it. Some men who do not know Mr. Seward well think he is arbitrary, dictatorial, domineering; whereas his temperament is peculiarly judicial and his appeals are always to the reason; his instincts, noble; his impulses, generous; all governed and modified by an illuminated intellect and a warm heart. George F. Seward is human and therefore neither infallible nor impossible, but his ideas of right and wrong would make good rules of conduct to hang in any man's business office.

I know that I have not followed the dictionary definition of "appreciation," but that is because the subject is too big for me.

W. A. Alexander

W. A. Alexander, of W. A. Alexander and Company, our general agents at Chicago, Illinois, wrote the following tribute:

A great man is dead!

He had the wisdom of a Confucius; the courage of a Napoleon; the heart of a Lincoln.

The old lion has at last been brought low and he lies in Woodlawn yonder under the sod awaiting the trumpet's call. He was your friend and mine; and what a thing it is to have been the friend of such a man! What a life was his! When but twenty-one, behind the great wall of China, alone, unafraid and undismayed, thousands of miles from his native land and from the powers that backed him, his courage, his judgment, and his great wisdom stood for something. When enemies assailed him and endeavored to wrest from him his vocation and his position, he fought the powers in Washington like a Caesar.

Soon after fortune placed him at the helm of our company, a crisis arose in its affairs and through the long day and night vigils under a ceaseless strain, he never flinched or swerved from his duty, and no matter which way the wind blew he kept her prow headed straight. He was fearless, and to those he loved and believed in, he was kind. To those of us who were before the mast with him he has left a heritage more precious than gold—the heritage of his example.

This afternoon as I sat in that magnificent temple of stone and steel, I felt much as I once did when I looked down upon the sarcophagus of Napoleon. Our Commander-in-Chief lay prone. Behind him, through the long train of years lay a record of good and pure deeds. His genius, somewhat unlike that of the old Napoleon, was constructive, not destructive; his was to lift up, not to tear down; his was to strengthen, never to weaken; and while he was building his or our structure, he was also pointing the way to others (many of them his most bitter competitors) to business success. When they trembled in the balance he could have pushed them over the precipice into the abyss and ignominy of complete failure; instead, he carried them along through his great knowledge and experience and forced them to listen to him. He was generous in victory; he was brave in defeat; he was kind in adversity; and turned a deaf ear to calumny and vituperation, holding up your hands and mine in spite of our enemies.

Men do not travel thousands of miles to pay their respects to men who make failures. In that temple of worship, sat prince and peasant side by side. Not an idle throng listening to the profound eulogy by Doctor Parkhurst, but earnest mourners; men and women of all classes, who had watched his career, crowded the church to the doors to pay their homage to a brave man who had heard his summons to come up higher.

When he heard the black wings of Death's Messenger, he folded his hands, bowed his great head, and, like the lion he was, lay down to die as he had lived—brave as a lion and true as steel.

Edwin W. De Leon

Edwin W. DeLeon, president of the Casualty Company of America, New York City, wrote the following paragraph in an article in the "Financial Review" of the *New York Times* of January 9, 1910, entitled "Casualty Insurance in 1910":

No record of the year would be complete without a brief reference at least to the recent untimely death of George F. Seward, the Nestor of the casualty insurance companies in America. He was a man of strong convictions, resolute will, and sound judgment, and he combined with these characteristics a kindly heart. His loss is more keenly felt and greatly deplored at this time, when men of mature experience, high purpose, and recognized ability are so much needed to help solve the great problems confronting the casualty insurance companies.

H. D. Lyman

H. D. Lyman, president of the American Surety Company, New York City, wrote the following lines:

I became acquainted with George F. Seward when he was appointed vice-president of the Fidelity & Casualty Company in the year 1887, but did not come to know him well until he succeeded to the presidency of the company after the decease of William M. Richards in 1892. Mr. Seward was an aggressive competitor in the various lines of casualty insurance, but his adversaries did not permit that fact to lessen their respect and esteem for him. He held their regard by reason of his ability, deference to others in business conferences, courtliness, and uprightness of character.

Kimball C. Atwood

Kimball C. Atwood, president of the Preferred Accident Insurance Company, New York City, wrote as follows:

It has been my privilege and pleasure to know Mr. Seward for many years; and to know him was to admire his sincerity, intelligence, progressiveness, and exceptionally vigorous personality. In his sudden death casualty underwriters have lost one of their strongest and ablest men.

William F. Moore

William F. Moore, president of the New Amsterdam Casualty Company, New York City, expressed himself as follows:

The report of the death of Mr. Seward came as a shock to his many friends in the insurance fraternity. We were all aware of his serious illness, but I can hardly think that any of us expected so sudden an ending. To me Mr. Seward's death is a personal loss. I have been intimately acquainted with him for over twenty years, and, during the early years of my insurance life when I was connected with the Fidelity & Casualty Company, I came in close daily contact with him and learned to appreciate his worth. To those who knew him well he was always the big-hearted, kindly gentleman. To the insurance fraternity he was the intellectual giant, a man with clear reasoning powers, a judicial mind and withal indomitable courage. His work was not confined to insurance alone. He found time to devote to commercial pursuits, to civic affairs, and to literature. His interest in affairs never lagged, and his death "in the harness" leaves a blank that will, perhaps, never be filled. Mr. Seward was a member of nearly all the casualty insurance associations of this city, and was looked upon as the dean of casualty insurance. His death will cause much sorrow in the whole insurance fraternity.

William B. Joyce

William B. Joyce, president of the National Surety Company, New York City, paid the following tribute:

Mr. Seward was the greatest casualty underwriter the world has seen. He was a great general, he made his moves deliberately and diplomatically. His ideas and ideals were of a high character. In his relations and associations with other underwriters and companies he was guided always by a sterling integrity.

William T. Woods

William T. Woods, president of Lloyds Plate Glass Insurance Company, New York City, wrote as follows:

In the death of Mr. Seward the various lines of casualty insurance have certainly suffered a great loss, and I think he was looked upon, particularly by accident and liability managers as a pilot. Only a few days ago, in a conversation with a prominent liability man, in speaking of Mr. Seward, he said that Mr. Seward had done more for employers' liability insurance than any other man he knew of. Mr. Seward was a remarkable man in many ways, and while during my long acquaintance with him I recognized he had a kind heart, still, to many who did not know him well, this may probably not have been observed. He will certainly be greatly missed in the casualty field, and the company he built to such grand proportions will forever stand as a monument to his great ability.

William M. Tomlins, Jr.

William M. Tomlins, Jr., president of the Empire State Surety Company, New York City, wrote as follows:

Mr. Seward was a man who made himself felt in casualty insurance circles, a man whose deeds in life will long be remembered. I regarded Mr. Seward as the dean of casualty men, not merely because of years of service but on account of his peculiar attainments, and I can think of no one who can exactly fill the vacancy caused by his death.

Eugene H. Winslow

Eugene H. Winslow, president of the Metropolitan Casualty Insurance Company, New York City, paid the following tribute:

Through business contact, it was my privilege to observe the varying experiences which he passed through unflinchingly in his strife for the great success which finally crowned his efforts in behalf of the company which he adorned as a man of affairs.

He was a man of rare mental attainments. He had an analytical mind which made his reasoning convincing. He was an executive in the broadest sense. He was constructive always, and his work bore evidence of the master hand in conception and execution. He builded not for a day but for all time.

When men of such exceptional ability are removed from life's activities, the business world feels the loss keenly and differences of thought and opinion are swept aside and friend and foe, alike, unite in a fitting recognition of their great achievements.

E. E. Clapp & Company

E. E. Clapp, of E. E. Clapp & Company, New York City, our general agents, wrote as follows:

The death of President George Frederick Seward comes as a great shock to all those who knew him. Those who had known him longest admired and loved him the most. After long diplomatic service to his country, Mr. Seward became vice-president of The Fidelity & Casualty Company in 1887, and six years later became, and has ever since been, its president. Mr. Seward's success in building up the company was so marked, his business ability so great, that the company speedily took first rank among similar institutions, and Mr. Seward was recognized as the foremost authority on casualty insurance in the United States. He was a man of broad mind, an experienced, prudent, and careful underwriter. His opinions were deliberate and free from prejudice, and were respected by all. He was not only a great leader, but a warm friend and of a charming personality. Every official, every agent, and every employee of the company deeply feels his loss.

Among his many notable traits, none stood out more prominently than his simple, modest, unassuming nature, and his intense, unwavering loyalty, both to his friends and to his principles and what he felt to be the right. His erudition, his great depth of thought, his wide grasp of affairs, his fifty years' diplomatic and business experience, and his remarkable magnanimity and nobility of character made him, indeed, a rare man amongst men.

Charles D. Lakey

In his paper of December 2, 1910, Charles D. Lakey, editor and proprietor of *Insurance* and for many years a friend of Mr. Seward, wrote the following editorial of appreciation:

That great man George F. Seward has passed into the life beyond, leaving a trail of light as he disappeared from mortal view. He went down like a shock of corn fully ripe. He had lived his season out.

When a man reaches his threescore years and ten, we are accustomed to think of him as having filled out his working day. The time limit has arrived. Let him stop. Nobody spoke thus of this man. At seventy, he was young. There was no trace of cloud shadow on his scintillant brain. As an organizer, manager, and leader, he was all he had ever been. There was no lack of vitality in the real man; only the shadow of him, the physical body, the house he dwelt in had begun to tire and give way. That was all.

For nearly a period of fifty years I have known the noted managers of the great business of insurance; Phelps, Crowell, Hope, Winston, Hyde, Beers, Greene, and McCall. These were giants. They put in foundations, and under their supervision indestructible walls were carried up. But this man stood head and shoulders with the best of them.

As an organizer he was supreme. He knew men. He believed in men. He trusted men. He had no occasion for rebuilding. The man put into place stayed. He stayed because he fitted the place.

The story of the Fidelity and Casualty, if carefully written up, would be found interesting. It began under conditions more or less depressing. It wrought in the twilight. There came on it the flash of a single mind and it rounded out into power.

We have not the intention here to amplify on what Mr. Seward did. We could speak of his long service for the United States Government in China. Here we think of him as he was, and as he is. A man. A noble specimen of manhood.

In the business of accident underwriting Mr. Seward was a master. In deliberative gatherings where important questions came up for discussion, men waited for his opinion. His was the last word. There was little to be said after he had presented his views.

The warm blood of human sympathy ran red in the veins of this man. It was much to be able

Reproduced from a recent Painting by William V. Schevill

1. View of Holcomb's Rock plant of Virginia Electrolytic Co., taken from east bank of the James River Mr. Seward owned this plant.
2. Interior of Power House at Holcomb's Rock, Va., showing six 250 K. W. dynamos used in electric smelting.
3. One thousand Horse Power Ferro-silicon Furnace at Holcomb's Rock

to say of him that he was your friend. He was a friend indeed.

I recall fragments of time spent with him, brief spaces of sunshine, moments snatched from hours of business pressure, and they will go with me to the end. He is mourned by the humblest worker in the great company he led to victory. There, I lay these words on the coffin that holds the cold clay. They are just a memory and regret. The man lives on. The great soul does not die.

MR. SEWARD'S VIRGINIA ENTERPRISE

The three views given on the opposite page show the Holcomb's Rock plant of Mr. Seward's enterprise, the Virginia Electrolytic Company.

This was a unique business, being the first electric smelting plant in the United States. Here was made all of the ferrochrome which went into United States projectiles during the Spanish War; much of the ferro-chrome which went into battle-ship armor of the United States Navy; and much of the ferro-chrome which went into Russian battle-ship armor before the Russian-Japanese War.

Mr. Seward acquired the ownership of the Virginia Electrolytic Co. and its Holcomb's Rock plant in 1906 from the Willson Aluminum Company, of which he was the first president and a large stockholder. The business of the company has since been carried on by his son, Geo. O. Seward, ably assisted by Mr. Franz von Kugelgen, the manager at Holcomb's Rock.

The plant at Holcomb's Rock consists of flowage rights to the entire capacity of the James River at that point, a dam, canal, power-house, furnace house, and numerous factory buildings, a store, hotel, and houses and cottages.

The electrical installation aggregates 2,000 horse-power and the current generated therefrom is all used in smelting metals in large electric furnaces by processes devised by the company.

TRIBUTES FROM THE PRESS

The press in general, and the insurance press in particular, took notice of Mr. Seward's death, and many of them printed eulogies upon his strong character and high purposes in life. Nearly a hundred such eulogies have been brought to our attention. Space, however, will admit of our quoting from only a few of them, as follows:

Editorial from New York Evening Post

"The death of George F. Seward removes a citizen of whom New York could well be proud. An insurance-company president who knew precisely what answer to give to grafters and political blackmailers, he was, wherever he went, a standing refutation of the stupid charge that all New York business men in high positions are there merely to subvert the liberties of the people or to make money illegally. But Mr. Seward was far more than a mere business man. He was a diplomat of experience, great skill, and wide vision. As consul, consul-general, and minister to Korea and China for nineteen years, Mr. Seward knew the East as did few Americans. And far from having any contempt for the Oriental, he brought back from China a profound respect for the Chinese, and an ever-ready indignation at their bad treatment by his country and his countrymen. His book, "Chinese Immigration," is to-day invaluable because of its profound knowledge and its sturdy insistence upon fair play, while at the same time a sorry record of American faithlessness as to word and treaty. In the Chamber of Commerce and other important civic bodies, Mr. Seward was ever listened to with profound respect as a wise, far-sighted councillor, who could never be swayed by any narrow considerations of locality or politics." (Nov. 29, 1910.)

Editorial from Brooklyn Daily Eagle

"George F. Seward, who died Sunday, was a little over 70. He was a nephew of William H. Seward. Abraham Lincoln, at the uncle's request, appointed the nephew to a position abroad. Subsequent Presidents advanced him in the service until he became our minister to China. In every diplomatic place he proved himself to a be a man of ability, wisdom, and aggressive integrity.

His subsequent experience in the headship of insurance companies indicated his breadth of mind, hatred of corruption, and courageous opposition to political highwaymen. His death will be sincerely regretted, for he was a strong man in a blatant land.

All the Sewards deserved well of America. The great Secretary needs no praise. Frederick his son, was a judicious statesman, Clarence A. Seward, a nephew, was a great lawyer, and George F. Seward, just dead, maintained the distinction of the name for capacity, integrity, and courage." (Nov. 29, 1910.)

Weekly Underwriter

"Mr. Seward will be missed from the insurance business because his interest in its welfare was so active that he was continuously at the front. That interest was not confined to his special line of insurance, for he wrote and spoke upon taxation, supervision, and kindred themes for the whole business. In casualty insurance he was the most forceful, clearsighted and alert of its exponents. There was no phase of the business with which his intellect did not grapple and always with success. We can appreciate the sense of loss which must prevail among his associates as they realize that his counsel and co-operation are no longer theirs, and that there is a vacancy that cannot again be wholly filled. They have well expressed it in their memorial allusions to the 'commanding position' he occupied in the business through his 'industry, intelligence and skill'; his 'exceeding energy and unusual mental attainments.' Mr. Seward was really a great man. He created an example toward which his fellow underwriters can aspire." (Dec. 3, 1910.)

United States Review

"By the death of George F. Seward, president of The Fidelity and Casualty Company, the world loses a man of large mind, broad sympathy, scholarly attainments and vigorous activity, the country a useful and patriotic citizen, and casualty insurance and suretyship a company official whose dominant activity made the company large and highly successful and made it stand for much that is best in both lines of business. He was always a stanch defender of insurance, and in its advocacy wielded a trenchant pen." (Dec. 1, 1910.)

IN MEMORIAM GEORGE FREDERICK SEWARD

*I give the strain in bated breath
As mother lulls a darling child,
For him who sleeps the sleep of death,
And in the path of honor toiled.*

Lightly lie the turf upon him, noble manhood he possessed,
  He of Casualty was master, let us sing him to his rest,
Friend of long ago remembered, you were girl—a stripling I,
  When he took our hearts to China and made history at Shanghai.

Well-beloved of Chinese Gordon, we recall the stress and storm
  Of the rising of the Taipings, like a locust-cloud enorm,
We behold, as in a vista, Ward and Seward in that fray,
  When the meteor flag of England and Old Glory held the day.

We recall how well in Siam, lion-hearted, suave and bland,
  Disentangled he the treaty 'twixt his country and that land,

East he led the course of empire, taught his countrymen to say:
  "Better all those years of Seward left the cycle of Cathay."

Then with honors full upon him, when some count their life-work done,
  He found other worlds to conquer, greater victories to be won,
Black Horse Cavalry engaged him, underwriters bond and free;
  In his life's success INSURANCE—President of the "F. and C."

This his work shall stand forever, finding aye a broader field,
  Reaping yet a grander harvest, richer years and riper yield,
Searching out new plans of venture of indemnity for man,
  Conquering and yet to conquer in the underwriting van.

Come then, goddess of the Record, Clio, write the story down,
  Lay upon his brow the laurel, crown him with the victor's crown,
It is finished—His great spirit has passed hence beyond the gates
  To receive his compensation where the Chief Adjuster waits.

—*George Moffat in Insurance Index, Dec. 1910.*

ADDRESS OF REV. CHARLES H. PARKHURST, D.D.

There is one singular fact connected always with the going out from our midst of one with whom we have been more or less closely associated, and that is this: that there is no time when the character, the outlines of the personality of individuals, becomes so distinct to us, so definitely formed before our mental vision and our heart vision as when they have just gone away from us. While they are with us, to a certain extent their own actions, their own words, their own exploits come between us and their own personal character; but when they are gone, we think less about what they have done, less about what they have said, less about their achievements, and more about what they were personally. The reality of their own personal being becomes singularly disclosed to us. When a man is alive we estimate him by the size of the deed that he has accomplished; we estimate him by the length and breadth of the words that he has uttered, if he be a speaker; and we are very apt to measure him by the amount of his pecuniary possessions; but when he is gone, what we think of is the man that was back of these outward manifestations. It always seems to be folly on an occasion of this kind to give what might be called a biographical sketch of the man's life. It is the man we are thinking about; it is the man, Mr. Seward, that you are thinking about this afternoon. You are feeling back through the avenue, through the channel of the things he has done, the kind words he has spoken, the achievements of his life; you are thinking back through those channels, back to their reality, to the man Seward himself.

Now, I am not proposing—it would be out of taste, it would be inconsistent, I am sure, with his own taste and the taste of his friends, if I were to eulogize him; but there is one thing I want to say about him. It is a great thing for a man in these days and in these times to be able to stand strong, immovable, untouched by the current, the rapid current, of the times in which he lives. Mr. Seward has demonstrated the fact, that some have been questioning, that a man can be in the insurance business and still be an honest man, and that he was too firmly morally grounded to be swerved from considerations that militate against strict and straight morality. It is rather the custom of the pulpit to say vituperative things about men on the street, but it is very cheap, and, I believe, very unjust. Of course there are some dishonest ones, but one dishonest man counts more in the press and in the common speech of people than the other ninety-nine men who go along quietly and steadily minding their business, doing that which is right and standing antagonistic to that which is evil and thus indicating the possibility of the man who is thoroughly grounded, the possibility of such a one standing up firm and strong.

Now, society is divided into two classes. The first class is composed of those who are tending to lift the community, society, the state, business, and all the rest higher; the other class is composed of those who are depressing society and lowering the tone of society either by positive acts or by negative indifference. Now, I doubt—from all I can gather—I doubt if there be one in this large and significant audience which is in itself a wonderful tribute to the manhood, to the Christian manhood, of the man who has gone—I doubt if there is one here who would hesitate to say that the tone of society, the tone of those in the midst of whom he has moved, in the midst of the circles where he has been so efficient—I doubt if there is one who will question my statement in saying that he has lifted the tone of society and business and has thus become a benefactor to his people and on the side of the Lord as against being on the other side. For there are only two classes, my friends, in the world; there are those who lift up and there are those who tear down; and, unless I am absolutely mistaken, and relying upon the unanimous testimony which has come to me in the last few days, Mr. Seward was an uplifter; and to those who have come into personal touch with him along social lines, along business lines, along foreign political lines, I believe there is not one but that is stronger and has a greater respect for what is right and true and steadfast because of the inspiration of his life.

Now, that is a good deal to say. It is a great thing to be a positive man on the right side; it is a great thing to be a man of that strength and wealth of character that is capable of putting its impress, its permanent impress for good on those who are younger or older than he; and Mr. Seward has touched men in a very great variety of ways. He demonstrates the fact that a man may be a thorough, substantial, business man and yet have a heart that is too large to be confined within the limitations of business and a mind too broad to be restrained within the confines of ordinary secular employment; and so also, in his consular and ambassadorial days, he put his touch, his spiritual finger, on thousands and thousands of lives. The wonderful thing about such a life as Mr. Seward's is that when the spiritual touch is once put on it is never removed; those things do not go out. A strong, great, sweet, well-balanced character writes itself indelibly upon the lives of others. And so, to-day, while people may not be conscious of it, while some of you who have come into close business relations, either as his colleagues or as his subordinates, may not be conscious of the fact, there is a writing on your mind, there is an inscription on your heart, there is an impulse communicated to your lives that you owe to him, and it is going to stay there. Men write their own epitaphs. People who require to have an epitaph written for them are mightily unfortunate. Usually those who write an epitaph for another write but one; but those who write their own epitaph write hundreds and thousands of epitaphs, and these epitaphs are in your souls, my good friends, you who have come into touch with him.

I think it is well to make much of those who go out from us, to cherish their remembrance, to brood over their lives. It is too easy in these rapid, hurricane days, to forget those that pass out of our sight. In a way we retain them, though it may be unconsciously; but I believe it would be more just to ourselves and more just to others if we would foster our remembrance of them, keep them alive in our memory and foster the remembrance of what they have been to us, so that we may, after they have passed on, respire the atmosphere which they, in by-gone days, have created round about them. It is these men that can be counted on and that we can tie to who are the safety of society. They may not make a great deal of noise in the world, but it is these men who are reliable. Paul said a great thing when he said "Stand, Stand." The hardest thing a man can do sometimes is simply to stand and buffet the current that rolls down against him. Mr. Seward was a man who stood. Whether more or less demonstrative in his life, that signifies naught. Look into your watch and you find there a number of jewels scattered around through its structure. They do not make any noise and they are not there for any movement that they make; but the stability of the fine machinery and the reliability of the watch depends upon the stability of the bearings. Now, these men are the bearings upon which the machinery of society and of business may be said to play. The security of the state, of society, of business, depends on the fact of their stability. It is, I believe, because Mr. Seward was a living, beaming illustration of this principle of the jewel that his life will work upon you with blessed, invigorating power, a power conveyed to you through the privilege you have had coming into association with him in relations of business and friendship.

May I read in closing a few lines from Thanatopsis, lines with which most of you are doubtless familiar:

"The golden sun,
The planets, all the infinite host of heaven,
Are shining on the sad abodes of death,
Through the still lapse of ages. All that tread
The globe are but a handful to the tribes
That slumber in its bosom.—Take the wings
Of morning, pierce the Barcan wilderness,
Or lose thyself in the continuous woods
Where rolls the Oregon, and hears no sound
Save his own dashings—yet the dead are there;
And millions in those solitudes, since first
The flight of years began, have laid them down
In their last sleep—the dead reign there alone.
So shalt thou rest; and what if thou withdraw
In silence from the living, and no friend
Take note of thy departure? All that breathe
Will share thy destiny. The gay will laugh
When thou art gone, the solemn brood of care
Plod on, and each one as before will chase
His favorite phantom; yet all these shall leave
Their mirth and their employments, and shall come
And make their bed with thee. As the long train
Of ages glides away, the sons of men—
The youth in life's fresh spring and he who goes
In the full strength of years, matron and maid,
The speechless babe and the gray-headed man—
Shall one by one be gathered to thy side,
By those who in their turn shall follow them.

So live, that when thy summons comes to join
The innumerable caravan which moves
To that mysterious realm where each shall take
His chamber in the silent halls of death,
Thou go not, like the quarry-slave at night,
Scourged to his dungeon; but, sustained and
    soothed
By an unfaltering trust, approach thy grave
Like one who wraps the drapery of his couch
About him, and lies down to pleasant dreams."

Madison Square Presbyterian Church, New York, November 30, 1910